BRANCH LINE TO SHREWSBURY

Vic Mitchell and Keith Smith

MP Middleton Press

First published January 1991

ISBN 0 906520 86 X

© Middleton Press 1991

Design - Deborah Goodridge
Laser typesetting - Barbara Mitchell

Published by Middleton Press
Easebourne Lane
Midhurst
West Sussex
Tel: (0730) 813169

Printed & bound by Biddles Ltd,
Guildford and Kings Lynn

CONTENTS

ACKNOWLEDGEMENTS

We are immensely grateful to those mentioned in the photograph credits for the additional information and help so freely given. Much assistance has also been received from Mrs J.E. Baker, C.Caddy, K.Catchpole, J.Clarke, D.Greenwood, J.Miller, P.Shaw, D.Smith, G.T.V.Stacey, E.Staff, N.Stanyon, Miss M. Wheeller, M.Wright, T.Wright and our ever helpful wives. To all these, we extend our deep gratitude.

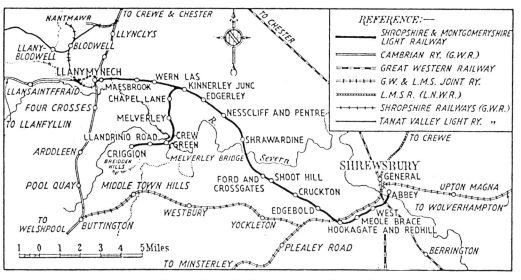

Map to show the former ownership of the railways adjacent to the Shropshire & Montgomeryshire Light Railway.
(Railway Magazine)

HISTORICAL BACKGROUND

The Shropshire & Montgomeryshire Light Railway was created on part of the route of the defunct Potteries, Shrewsbury & North Wales Railway. This line was to have linked the places mentioned but never did so, merely carrying local passengers on double track between Shrewsbury and Llanymynech, from 13th August 1866. There were also goods lines to Llanyblodwell and to Criggion, then known as Breidden. Freight services were extended to Nantmawr in 1872. The single lines to Criggion and to Llanyblodwell received passenger services in about 1871 but a precise date is difficult to establish.

Long known as "The Potts", the company struggled on until 3rd December 1866, when the bailiffs moved in, traffic ceasing on 21st December of that year.

The Shrewsbury - Llanymynech section reopened as a single line in December 1868, the Criggion service commencing in June 1871 and that to Llanyblodwell following in 1872. Recurring financial problems resulted in a receiver being appointed in 1877 and total closure taking place on 22nd June 1880. The decaying rolling stock was auctioned eight years later.

In 1881, the Cambrian Railway undertook to maintain and operate the line west of Llanymynech, this section of the route reopening in 1886 and eventually coming under the control of the GWR.

A new company - Shropshire Railways - took control of the route east of Llanymynech in 1890 and relaid the track. Financial irregularities resulted in receivership once again and the buildings and other structures fell into ruin once more.

Following local pressure for the reopening of the line, the Shropshire & Montgomeryshire Light Railway Co Ltd was formed in 1907, largely financed by local councils. The Light Railway Order was issued in February 1909 and work soon commenced on clearing the linear jungle and replacing all the sleepers.

The engineer to the new company (and one of its directors) was H.F.Stephens, then well known as promoter and builder of light railways. Gaining the rank of Lieutenant Colonel during World War I, he subsequently

1. Few photographs were taken during "The Potts" era and those that were have already been published. This view of Crossgates is typical of the melancholy scene to be found throughout the system during the period of dormancy, when all sleepers rotted and nature took over. A "skeleton" staff was retained to maintain fences - a legal obligation. (R.S.Carpenter coll.)

2. Holman Fred Stephens established his offices at Tonbridge from where he managed light railways as different and widely separated as the Festiniog and the East Kent. He is seen embarking on an inspection of the new S&M, which was to later benefit (?) from his policy of moving locomotives (and nameplates) from one line to another. (Col. Stephens Railway Archives)

was known simply as Colonel Stephens, as his empire of minor railways grew to seventeen in number.

The formal reopening took place at Shrewsbury Abbey Foregate on 13th April 1911 but a derailment on the following day closed the line again for 48 hours. The Criggion branch reopened for freight on 21st February 1912 and for passengers the following August.

The sparseness of habitation and competition from road transport resulted in the early reduction in passenger services. On the Criggion branch, these ran on Saturdays only from 1928 and regular services over the entire system were withdrawn on 6th November 1933. Only holiday excursions remained and even these were abolished in 1937, leaving only one freight service, weekdays only.

On 1st September 1939, the railway came under the control of the Railway Executive, due to the impending war. One consequence of this was that an annual profit of £1 was guaranteed. At this time there was a staff of about 40.

In May 1940, the directors proposed closure of the line between Kinnerley and Meole Brace but problems arose over the redirection of quarry traffic via Llanymynech.

On 1st June 1941, the Shrewsbury-Llanymynech section was requisitioned by the War Department to serve the extensive munition depots being laid out in the area. The line was extensively relaid largely with concrete sleepers, and operated by military personnel, up to twelve locomotives being in steam simultaneously. The regular civilian freight train continued to operate.

In 1947, the line was given W D Civilian status and upon nationalisation in 1948, only the Criggion branch became the responsibility of British Railways (Western Region). Public freight services were withdrawn from this branch on 2nd May 1949, but stone traffic continued.

The WD relinquished control in 1960, the Criggion branch having closed in December 1959. The last regular train for civilian workers ran on 26th February 1960 and an enthusiasts' special followed on 31st March of that year.

The line was transferred to BR who became responsible for its demolition. All track was lifted in 1962, apart from the oil depot sidings at Shrewsbury, which had been given a new connection to BR in 1960. These finally closed in July 1988 and were lifted early in 1990.

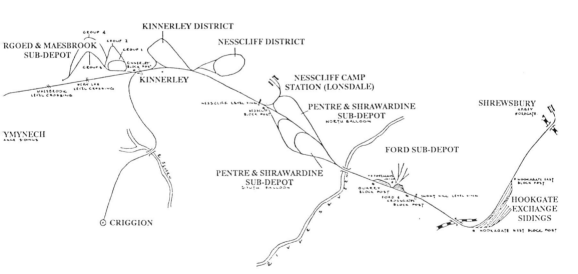

Diagram of the War Department Depot at its optimum in the latter part of World War II. Numerous sidings served 205 ammunition store buildings, the system being operated by No. 1 Group of the Royal Engineers. The mileage of the railway increased from 28 to 78 miles during Army use.

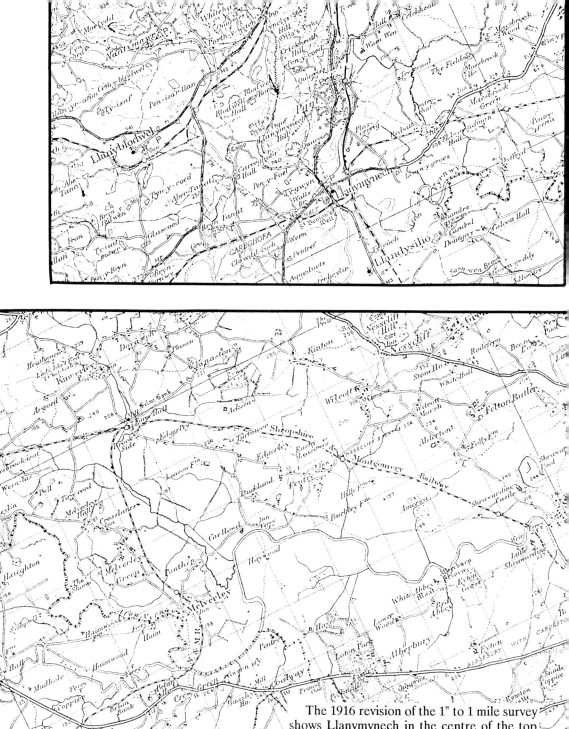

The 1916 revision of the 1" to 1 mile survey shows Llanymynech in the centre of the top map, which is continuous with the main map. On this part, Criggion is lower left and Shrewsbury is upper right. Later road improvements have been incorporated.

GEOGRAPHICAL SETTING

The entire route and its branch is closely associated with the River Severn and its tributaries, notably the Afon Vyrnwy, which is close to the station at Llanymynech and enters the Severn just above Melverley Bridge. The limestone quarries of Llanymynech Hill once generated traffic for the PS&NWR but the mineral traffic on the S&M was limited to Greenstone from Breidden Hill at Criggion. This hard blue-green Dolerite is an ideal roadstone.

Most of the route crossed the Boulder Clay of the Severn Valley but east of Edgebold it was largely on gravel, underlying coal measures being a feature in the Meole Brace area.

The national boundary runs north-south along the main street of Llanymynech, the station thus being in England. Only two miles of the S&M was in Montgomeryshire, this being the section between Criggion and Crew Green, where coal was still worked at the time of the opening of "The Potts".

All maps are to the scale of 25" to 1 mile, unless otherwise stated. Unfortunately, most of the system was not surveyed during the life of the S&M and so earlier editions are generally shown.

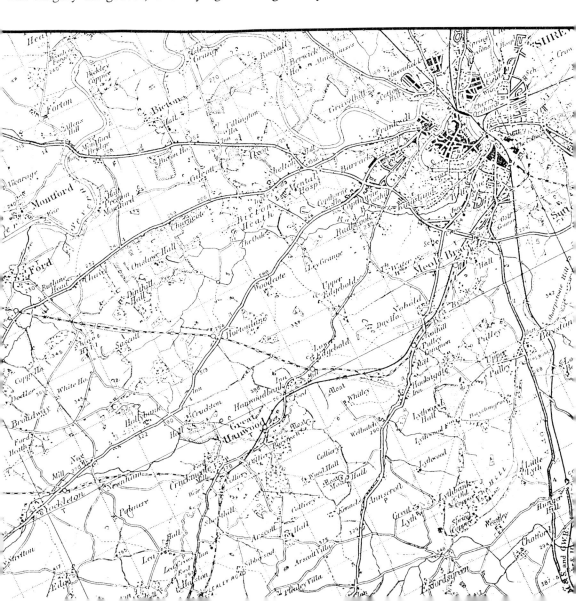

TRAFFIC

Passengers -	1879	1913	1919	1925	1932	1938
1st Class	-	80	657	16	-	-
3rd Class	73601	65864	57146	30245	9142	-
Workmen	-	-	8073	9012	-	-
Seasons 1st	-	-	1	-	-	-
Seasons 3rd	3	4	6	16	-	-
Merchandise	5046	1162	5514	1824	845	948
Minerals	23837	14214	44131	63095	79611	16931
Livestock	?	941	3965	4731	579	66

In the summary table above, the figures for merchandise and minerals refer to tons originating on the line. The returns for 1919 also showed 13 tons of coal loaded and 2280 prisoners carried.

The drop in merchandise after 1919 followed the release of over 60,000 ex-Army lorries onto the roads of Britain, where previously there had been only about 2000.

In the years 1942-44 an average of 45,000 tons of general goods was carried per annum. Military traffic peaked at 349,986 tons in 1943.

Between 1927 and 1948, an average of over 1000 tons of sugar beet was despatched per annum by the S&M, destined for the works at Allscott and mainly from Ford and Shrawardine.

The table below shows a sudden increase in coal traffic in 1922, which is proably due to the opening of the coal yard at Abbey Foregate. The peak in mineral traffic in 1930-31 resulted from the demand for stone during the construction of the East Lancs Road between Liverpool and Manchester.

Carriage of Goods. (in tons)

Date	Minerals	Gen.Merch.	Coal,coke etc.	Total Carried	Total Originating
1911	6306	1451	-	7757	?
1912	16124	3704	-	19827	?
1913					
1918	No statistics published during the Great War.				
1919	45340	5804	13	51157	?
1920	54126	4299	-	58425	?
1921	41423	2014	45	43482	
1922	60895	9005	8828	78728	60031
1923	53764	8013	9275	71052	54268
1924	64352	9299	9236	82977	63397
1925	63177	8911	9872	86960	64919
1926	48371	8447	6300	63118	47636
1927	59626	6203	7743	73572	58327
1928	60873	5802	7660	74335	58701
1929	66209	5719	8588	80516	65295
1930	101526	4982	8143	114651	99724
1931	145472	4703	7873	158048	143894
1932	82159	6201	7624	95984	80463
1933	34511	5340	7145	46996	30676
1934	25308	8196	8290	41794	23449
1935	43611	10721	9631	63963	42938
1936	26105	11572	9423	47100	24971
1937	22869	11742	9551	44162	21524
1938	18292	11223	7562	37077	17915

Date.	Total Loco Milage.	Rail Motor Milage.	Total Number of Passengers Carried.	Number of Pass. Originating on the System.
1911	?	-	42003	
1912	?	-	64094	
1913	No statistics published until after the Great War.			
1919	62766	-	68156	
1920	59786	-	74702	
1921	54316	-	67166	
1922	71234	-	52583	52289
1923	77656	-	50122	49730
1924	79554	17642	47526	45571
1925	76820	18033	39273	38182
1926	61509	23544	27892	27821
1927	63156	32848	22143	22102
1928	58748	35967	19806	19719
1929	58513	27505	16644	16555
1930	57990	19723	13717	13637
1931	56638	17536	11358	11352
1932	42551	7871	9142	9116
1933	23455	5146	3280	3248
1934	17194	2548	604	
1935	19095	2392	474	
1936	14907	204	212	
1937	14535	-	164	
1938	14026	-	262	

Date	Total Passenger Receipts	Total Goods Receipts	Total Receipts	W'king Expendt.	NET RECEIPTS
1911	1277	648	2023	1560	£ 463
1912	1688	1911	3848	3062	£ 786
1913					
1918	No statistics published during the Great War.				
1919					
1922	2543	12710	15384	14138	£ 1246
1923	2242	12875	15074	13443	£ 1631
1924	1931	11474	13461	12146	£ 1315
1925	1712	11668	13471	12279	£ 1192
1926	1198	8747	9992	10340	£- 348
1927	1118	10062	11252	9942	£ 1310
1928	917	9312	10276	8783	£ 1493
1929	772	9593	10416	9009	£ 1407
1930	559	12641	13244	11679	£ 1565
1931	524	15885	16499	14839	£ 1660
1932	345	9895	10349	10060	£- 289
1933	173	5062	5334	6150	£- 816
1934	109	4233	4401	5510	£-1109
1935	151	6046	6268	6173	£ 95
1936	147	5105	5329	6064	£- 735
1937	196	4629	4950	6361	£-1141
1938	134	3937	4134	5712	£-1578

PASSENGER SERVICES

The initial timetable for the PS&NWR showed five weekday and two Sunday trains. Upon reopening in 1868, this was reduced to three and one respectively, with an additional journey each way on Wednesdays, Thursdays and Saturdays.

Following reopening in 1911, there was a basic service of three weekday and two Sunday trains, the latter being withdrawn permanently in 1916. For much of the early 1920s there were four weekday journeys. The variation in extra Saturday trains are shown in the specimen timetables included in this album.

The final timetable (from 6th February 1933) comprised two return journeys, departing from Shrewsbury at 7.30 and 10.15 am only, with two additional return trips on Saturdays to Melverley.

Criggion Branch

From 1912 until 1915, there were four weekday trains, with one on Sundays. The latter was withdrawn in 1916 and the remaining service greatly reduced during the rest of World War I.

For most of the 1920s, there were only two regular journeys on weekdays and, in October 1928, this was reduced to Saturdays only. In October 1932, this was cut back to Melverley, owing to the condition of the viaduct.

LLANYMYNECH JUNCTION and SHREWSBURY.—Shropshire and Montgomeryshire.
Man. Director, Eng., and Loco. Supt., H. F. Stephens, Tonbridge, Kent.

(timetable — October 1911)

October 1911

(timetable — October 1914)

October 1914

(timetable — July 1919)

July 1919

Down.	mrn	mrn	mrn	mrn	aft	aft Except Saturdays.	aft Except Saturdays.	aft Saturdays only.	aft	aft
Abbey Station, ewsbury.......dep	....	....	9 35	....	1 30	....	3 5	3 30	4 20	6 45
ewsbury West......			c		c	....	c	....	c	c
le Brace...........			9 45		1 40	....	3 15	3 35	4 30	6 50
kagate...........			c		c	....	c	3 40	c	c
ebold...........			c		c	....	c	c	c	c
ckton *			c		c	....	c	c	c	....
l and Crossgates........			10 5		2 5	....	3 40	3 51	4 55	7 7
awardine...........			c		c	....	c	4 1		c
scliff and Pentre....			1020		2 20	....	c	4 6		7 25
nerley Junction arr.			1029		2 24	....	4 0	4 15		7 30
Kinnerley Junc. dep.	6 40	....	Third class only.	1045	Third class only.	4 5	....	4 16	Except Saturdays. Third class only.	....
Chapel Lane........	c	....		a		c	....	c		....
Melverley........	6 47	....		a		4 12	....	4 23		....
Crew Green A.....	6 52	....		a		4 17	....	4 30		....
Llandrinio Road...	7 0	....		a		4 22	....	4 40		....
Criggion.......arr.	7 5	....		1115		4 30	....	4 50		....
nerley Junction dep	....	7 30	1030	....	2 25	....	4 20	....		7 32
n Las..........	....	c	c	....	c	....	c	....		c
sbrook....|138,145	....	7 40	1040	....	c	....	4 30	....		7 40
ymynech 136, arr.	....	7 45	1045	....	2 40	....	4 40	....		7 45

Up.	mrn	mrn	aft Except Saturdays.	aft Saturdays only.	aft Except Saturdays.	aft Saturdays only.	aft Except Saturdays.	aft	aft
nymynech......dep	8 10	1125		....	3 0	3 10	....	5 25	8 10
sbrook...........	8 15	1132		....	c	c	....	c	8 15
n Las..........	c	c		....	c	c	....	c	a
nerley Junction arr.	8 28	1138		....	3 15	3 25	....	5 43	8 23
Criggion.......dep	8 0	Third class only.		1240	Third class only.		Third class only.	5 5	....
Llandrinio Road...	8 5			c				c	....
Crew Green A.....	8 10			c				5 12	....
Melverley........	8 17			c				5 16	....
Chapel Lane........	c			c				c	....
Kinnerley Junc. arr.	8 24			1 10				5 22	....
nerley Junction dep	8 30	1145	1 0	1 30	3 20		....	5 45	8 25
scliff and Pentre....	8 40	1153	1 10	1 38	3 25		....	5 52	d
awardine........	8 45	12 0	1 20	1 45	3 35		....	c	....
d and Crossgates * ..	8 55	1210	2 10	2 10	3 45		5 0	6 8	....
ckton..........	c	c	c	c	c		c	a	....
ebold..........	9 5	1220	c	c	c		c	c	....
kagate..........	9 10	1225	c	c	c		c	c	....
le Brace..........	9 15	1230	2 30	2 30	4 10	....	5 23	6 25	....
ewsbury West |384	c	c	....	c	....	....	....	c	....
ewsbury B382, arr.	9 25	1245	2 45	2 45	4 15	....	5 30	6 35	....

tember 1925

Down.	mrn Saturdays only.		mrn	mrn		aft	aft Thursdays only.		aft Saturdays only.	aft		aft Thursdays only.	aft
Abbey Station, Shrewsbury.......dep.	....	....	....	8 55	....	1 45	....	....	3 17	5 0	....	....	7 55
Shrewsbury West........	....	....	....	....	....	....	....	....	....	....	....	....	....
Meole Brace..........		....	....	9 5	....	1 55		....	3 27	5 9	....		8 5
Hookagate and Redhill.		....	....	Cc	....	Cc		....	Cc	Cc	....		Cc
Edgebold..........		....	....	Cc	....	2 5		....	Cc	5 20	....		8 15
Cruckton..........		....	....	Cc	....	Cc		....	Cc	Cc	....		Cc
Shoot Hill..........		....	....	Cc	....	Cc		....	Cc	Cc	....		Cc
Ford and Crossgates....		....	....	9 20	....	2 15		....	3 47	5 30	....		8 25
Shrawardine........		....	....	9 28	....	2 23		....	Cc	Cc	....		Cc
Nesscliff and Pentre....		....	....	9 35	....	2 30		....	4 2	5 45	....		8 40
Edgerley..........		....	....	Cc	....	Cc		....	Cc	Cc	....		Cc
Kinnerley Junction....		....	7 30	9 45	....	2 40		....	4 7	5 50	....		8 50
Kinnerley Junc. dep.	7 0	....				....	2 45	....	4 7	....	....	5 55	....
Chapel Lane........	Cc	....				....	Cc	....	Cc	....	....	Cc	....
Melverley..........	7 7	....				....	2 52	....	4 14	....	....	6 2	....
Crew Green A.....	7 12	....				....	Cc	....	Cc	....	....	6 7	....
Llandrinio Road...	7 17	....				....	3 2	....	4 24	....	....	6 12	....
Criggion.......arr.	7 25	....				....	3 10	....	4 32	....	....	6 20	....
Wern Las..........	....	....	Cc	Cc	....	Cc	....	....	....	Cc	....	....	Aa
Maesbrook....|138,145	....	....	7 40	9 55	....	2 45	....	....	....	5 55	....	....	Aa
Llanymynech 136, arr.	....	....	7 45	10 5	....	2 55	....	....	....	6 5	....	....	9 5

Up.	mrn	mrn		mrn	mrn		aft	aft	aft		aft	aft	aft	
Llanymynech......dep.	....	....	....	8 12	1117	....		....	3 52	....	....	....	6 40	....
Maesbrook..........				8 17	1122	....	Saturdays only.	....	3 57	....	....	....	6 45	....
Wern Las..........				Cc	Cc	....		....	Cc	....	....	....	Cc	....
Mls Criggion.......dep.	7 30	....	....			....		3 15	....	....	4 37	6 25	....	....
1 Llandrinio Road...	7 35	....	....			....		3 20	....	....	4 42	6 30	....	....
2 Crew Green A.....	Cc	....	....			....		Cc	....	....	Cc	Cc	....	....
5¼ Melverley........	7 45	....	....			....		3 30	....	....	4 52	6 40	....	....
6¼ Chapel Lane........	Cc	....	....			....		Cc	....	....	Cc	Cc	....	....
7¼ Kinnerley Junc. arr.	7 55	....	....			....		3 40	....	....	5 2	6 50	....	....
Kinnerley Junction....	Saturdays only.	8 0	....	8 35	1137	....	1 40	Thursdays only.	4 7	....	Saturdays only.	Thursdays only.	6 55	....
Edgerley..........		Cc	....	Cc	Cc	....	Cc		Cc	....			Cc	....
Nesscliff and Pentre....		8 8	....	8 45	1145	....	Cc		4 14	....			7 3	....
Shrawardine..........		8 15	....	Cc	1152	....	Cc		4 21	....			Cc	....
Ford and Crossgates....		8 25	....	9 20	12 2	....	2 15		4 31	....			7 20	....
Shoot Hill..........		Cc	....	Cc	Cc	....	Cc		Cc	....			Cc	....
Cruckton..........		Cc	....	Cc	Cc	....	Cc		Cc	....			Cc	....
Edgebold..........		8 35	....	Cc	1212	....	2 25		4 41	....			7 30	....
Hookagate and Redhill.		Cc	....	Cc	Cc	....	Cc		Cc	....			Cc	....
Meole Brace..........	....	8 45	....	9 40	1222	....	2 40		4 49	....	....	....	7 40	....
Shrewsbury West |488	....	....	....	....	....	....	....	....	....	....	....	....	....	....
Shrewsbury B486, arr.	....	8 50	....	9 55	1232	....	2 55	....	4 58	....	....	....	7 50	....

August 1928

Down.	mrn Saturdays only.	mrn		mrn	mrn		aft		aft Saturdays only.	aft
Abbey Station, ewsbury.......dep.	....	....	....	9 0	1030	....	1 45	....	3 17	5 0
ewsbury West........	....	....	....	Cc	Cc	....	Cc	....	Cc	Cc
le Brace..........		....	....	9 15	1040	....	1 55	....	3 27	5 9
kagate and Redhill.		....	....	Cc	Cc	....	Cc	....	Cc	Cc
ebold..........		....	....	Cc	1050	....	2 5	....	Cc	5 20
ckton..........		....	....	Cc	Cc	....	Cc	....	Cc	Cc
ot Hill..........		....	....	Cc	Cc	....	Cc	....	Cc	Cc
d and Crossgates....		....	....	9 30	1110	....	2 15	....	3 47	5 30
awardine..........		....	....	9 37	Cc	....	2 23	....	Cc	Cc
scliff and Pentre....		....	....	9 45	1125	....	2 30	....	4 2	5 45
erley..........		....	....	Cc	Cc	....	Cc	....	Cc	Cc
nerley Junction....		7 30	....	9 55	1135	....	2 40	....	4 7	5 50
Kinnerley Junc. dep.	7 0	....	....	....	....	....	....	....	4 7	....
Chapel Lane........	Cc	....	....	....	....	....	....	....	Cc	....
Melverley..........	7 7	....	....	....	....	....	....	....	4 14	....
Crew Green A.....	7 12	....	....	....	....	....	....	....	Cc	....
Llandrinio Road...	7 17	....	....	....	....	....	....	....	4 24	....
Criggion.......arr.	7 25	....	....	....	....	....	....	....	4 32	....
rn Las..........	....	Cc	....	Cc	....	....	Cc	....	....	Cc
sbrook....|138,145	....	7 40	....	10 5	....	....	2 45	....	....	5 55
nymynech 136, arr.	....	7 45	....	1015	....	....	2 55	....	....	6 5

Up.	mrn	mrn	mrn		mrn	aft Saturdays only.		aft	aft		aft
nymynech......dep.	....	....	8 7	....	1117		....	3 52	....	....	6 40
esbrook..........	....	....	8 12	....	1122		....	3 57	....	....	6 45
rn Las..........	....	....	Cc	....	Cc		....	Cc	....	....	Cc
Criggion......dep.	7 30	....	....	....	....		....	....	4 37	....	....
Llandrinio Road...	7 35	....	....	....	....		....	....	4 42	....	....
Crew Green A.....	Cc	....	....	....	....		....	....	Cc	....	....
Melverley..........	7 45	....		....	....		....	....	4 52	....	....
Chapel Lane........	Cc	....	....	....	....		....	....	Cc	....	....
Kinnerley Junc. arr.	7 55	....	....	....	....		....	....	5 2	....	....
nerley Junction....	Saturdays only.	8 0	8 30	....	1137	1 40	....	4 7	Saturdays only.	....	6 55
erley..........		Cc	Cc	....	Cc	Cc	....	Cc		....	....
scliff and Pentre....		8 8	8 37	....	1145	Cc	....	4 14		....	....
awardine..........		8 15	Cc	....	1152	Cc	....	4 21		....	....
d and Crossgates....		8 25	8 50	....	12 2	2 15	....	4 31		....	....
ot Hill..........		Cc	Cc	....	Cc	Cc	....	Cc		....	....
ckton..........		Cc	Cc	....	Cc	Cc	....	Cc		....	....
ebold..........		8 35	Cc	....	1212	2 25	....	4 41		....	....
kagate and Redhill.		Cc	Cc	....	Cc	Cc	....	Cc		....	....
le Brace..........	....	8 45	9 15	....	1222	2 40	....	4 49	....	....	....
ewsbury West |488	....	Cc	Cc	....	Cc	Cc	....	Cc	....	....	....
ewsbury B486, arr.	....	8 50	9 30	....	1232	2 55	....	4 58	....	....	....

vember 1930

Down.	mrn Saturdays only.	mrn		mrn	mrn		aft		aft Saturdays only.	aft Except Wednesdays.	aft Wednesdays only.	
Abbey Station, Shrewsbury.......dep.	....	....	....	9 0	10 0	....	1 45	....	3 17	5 30	6 20	....
Shrewsbury West......	....	....	....	Cc	Cc	....	Cc	....	Cc	Cc	Cc	....
Meole Brace..........		....	....	9 15	1015	....	2 0	....	3 27	5 40	6 30	....
Hookagate and Redhill.		....	....	Cc	Cc	....	Cc	....	Cc	Cc	Cc	....
Edgebold..........		....	....	Cc	1025	....	2 10	....	Cc	5 50	6 40	....
Cruckton..........		....	....	Cc	Cc	....	Cc	....	Cc	Cc	Cc	....
Shoot Hill..........		....	....	Cc	Cc	....	Cc	....	Cc	Cc	Cc	....
Ford and Crossgates....		....	....	9 30	1040	....	2 25	....	3 47	6 5	6 55	....
Shrawardine..........		....	....	9 37	Cc	....	Cc	....	Cc	Cc	Cc	....
Nesscliff and Pentre....		....	....	9 45	1055	....	2 40	....	4 2	6 20	7 10	....
Edgerley..........		....	....	Cc	Cc	....	Cc	....	Cc	Cc	Cc	....
Kinnerley Junction....		7 30	....	9 55	11 5	....	2 50	....	4 7	6 30	7 20	....
Kinnerley Junc. dep.	7 0	....	....	....	....	....	....	....	4 7	....	....	....
Chapel Lane........	Cc	....	....	....	....	....	....	....	Cc	....	....	....
Melverley..........	7 7	....	....	....	....	....	....	....	4 14	....	....	....
Crew Green A.....	7 12	....	....	....	....	....	....	....	Cc	....	....	....
Llandrinio Road...	7 17	....	....	....	....	....	....	....	4 24	....	....	....
Criggion.......arr.	7 25	....	....	....	....	....	....	....	4 32	....	....	....
Wern Las..........	....	Cc	....	Cc	....	....	Cc	....	....	Cc	Cc	....
Maesbrook....|138,145	....	7 40	....	10 5	....	....	2 55	....	....	6 40	7 30	....
Llanymynech 136, arr.	....	7 45	....	1015	....	....	3 5	....	....	6 50	7 40	....

Up.	mrn	mrn	mrn		mrn	aft Saturdays only.	aft Except Wednesdays.	aft Wednesdays only.	aft	aft Except Wednesdays.	aft Wednesdays only.
Llanymynech......dep.	....	....	8 7	....	1122		3 52	4 42	....	7 0	7 50
Maesbrook..........	....	....	8 12	....	1127		3 57	4 47	....	7 5	7 55
Wern Las..........	....	....	Cc	....	Cc		Cc	Cc	....	Cc	Cc
Mls Criggion.......dep.	7 30	....	....	....	....		....	....	4 37	....	....
1 Llandrinio Road...	7 35	....	....	....	....		....	....	4 42	....	....
2 Crew Green A.....	Cc	....	....	....	....		....	....	Cc	....	....
5¼ Melverley..........	7 45	....	....	....	....		....	....	4 52	....	....
6¼ Chapel Lane........	Cc	....	....	....	....		....	....	Cc	....	....
7¼ Kinnerley Junc. arr.	7 55	....	....	....	....		....	....	5 2	....	....
Kinnerley Junction....	Saturdays only.	8 0	8 30	....	1150	1 50	4 7	4 57	Saturdays only.	7 15	8 5
Edgerley..........		Cc	Cc	....	Cc	Cc	Cc	Cc		....	....
Nesscliff and Pentre....		8 8	8 37	....	12 0	Cc	4 17	5 7		....	....
Shrawardine..........		8 15	Cc	....	Cc	Cc	Cc	Cc		....	....
Ford and Crossgates....		8 25	8 50	....	1215	2 25	4 32	5 22		....	....
Shoot Hill..........		Cc	Cc	....	Ce	Cc	Cc	Cc		....	....
Cruckton..........		Cc	Cc	....	Cc	Cc	Cc	Cc		....	....
Edgebold..........		8 35	Cc	....	1225	2 35	4 42	5 32		....	....
Hookagate and Redhill.		Cc	Cc	....	Cc	Cc	Cc	Cc		....	....
Meole Brace..........	....	8 45	9 15	....	1235	2 50	5 0	5 50	....	....	....
Shrewsbury West |488	....	Cc	Cc	....	Cc	Cc	Cc	Cc	....	....	....
Shrewsbury B436, arr.	....	8 50	9 30	....	1250	3 5	5 20	6 10	....	....	....

April 1932

NOTES.

A Station for Alberbury, Coedway.

a Stops to set down.

B Abbey; bout ¼ mile to General Station.

c Stop when required.

d Will run to Nesscliff if required.

* "Halt" at Shoot Hill, between Cruckton and Ford and Crossgates.

LOCOMOTIVES

3. No. 1 *Gazelle* was built by Dodman & Co in Kings Lynn in 1893 for Mr William Burkitt, who was allowed to use it as personal transport by the GER and M&GNR. It is reputedly the smallest standard gauge locomotive built and is seen in its original 2-2-2 arrangement on test at Stow on 5th February 1893. Note the rear door and seats for four. (L.Darbyshire coll.)

4. Stephens bought *Gazelle* in 1911 and used it for passengers to Criggion in the form seen in the previous photograph. He soon sent it to Bagnalls for conversion to 0-4-2 and the fitting of a roof and exterior luggage rack for passenger benefit. He also used it for inspection purposes. It was regularly used on the Criggion branch, coupled to an ex-LCC horse-drawn tramcar, shorn of its platforms, stairs and upper deck seats.
(Colonel Stephens Railway Archives)

5.   The 5-ton locomotive had its wooden lagging exposed, when photographed on 28th May 1932.   The outer wheels were of the Mansell type, with teak segments between the rim and boss.   One of these was used as a pattern for the casting of the new driving wheels in 1911. In 1937, Stephens' successor, W.H.Austen, decided on rebuilding in the form seen in pictures nos. 54 and 70. During WWII, it served the Army as a regular early morning inspection unit and was sent to Longmoor in 1950, where it was on display. It is now to be seen in the Museum of Army Transport at Beverley. (H.C.Casserley)

6.   No. 2 *Hecate* was renamed *Severn* by Stephens in 1916 but the uncertain early history of this locomotive remains. Once thought to have been an 0-4-0 on the Shrewsbury & Hereford Railway, it now appears to have been built in Liverpool by Berry, Curtis and Kennedy in 1848 for the Shrewsbury & Chester Railway, where it ran as number 17 or 18, but without a cab. Another theory is that it was originally no.23 on the St. Helens Railway. (Colonel Stephens Railway Archives)

7. No. 2 was purchased in September 1911 and was in use until 1931. Photographed in 1932, it was cut up in 1937. The tank belonged to Terrier no. 8 *Dido*. Stephens also used the name *Hecate* on a massive new 0-8-0T on his K&ESR. (S.W.Baker)

8. No.3 *Hesperus* was built by Beyer Peacock for the LSWR in 1875 and it was one of a batch of eight 0-6-0s designed for use on the steeply graded and lightweight track of the Ilfracombe line. Stephens found them ideal for several of his lines, the S&M receiving three: No.3 (in use 1911-28 and 1938-39), no. 5 *Pyramus* (1914-1930) and no. 6 *Thisbe* (1916-34). (Colonel Stephens Railway Archives)

9. No. 4 *Morous*. This contractor's loco-motive emerged from Manning Wardle's Leeds works in 1866 and arrived on the S&M in 1910. The Colonel transferred it to his West Sussex Railway in 1924, where it was more successful and ran until closure of the line in 1935. (L.Darbyshire coll.)

10. *Walton Park* was a 1908 Hudswell Clarke product and was transferred in 1913 from the Weston, Cleveland & Portishead Railway, where Stephens was engineer and where there was a station after which it was named. No. 4 was its WC&PR number. In August 1916, it moved to the Colonel's East Kent Light Railway, where it remained until 1943. It avoided the cutter's torch until 1957. (Lens of Sutton)

11. No. 5 *Pyramus*. This engine and no. 6 *Thisbe* were built for the line in 1911 by Hawthorn Leslie, to Stephens' drawings. At 36 tons each, they proved too heavy for the track and were sold to the Woolmer Instructional Military Railway in 1914 - see our *Branch Lines to Longmoor*. Their names were transferred to two of the "Ilfracombe Goods" that replaced them. (R.C.Riley coll.)

12. No. 9 *Daphne*. Stephens favoured the former LBSCR Terriers but they were not often used on the S&M. No. 9 of 1880 build arrived in 1923 and was sold to the SR in 1938 for spares, after years of disuse. No. 8 *Dido* (in use 1923-30) and no. 7 *Hecate* (1921-30) were two other members of the class that were equally unsuccessful on the route. Rolt records that, owing to lack of injectors, they were prone to run short of water on rising gradients. This necessitated abandoning the train and going for a run to pump more water into the boiler. (J.A.G.Coltas)

13. Three ex-LNWR coal engines ("Colliers"), bearing the LMS numbers 8108, 8182 and 8236, were purchased in 1930, 1931 and 1932, respectively. They lasted until 1946, when they were ousted by the "Austerity" 0-6-0STs, although they were not cut up until 1950. No. 8108 went into Kinnerley shed in 1936 for a major overhaul which lasted until April 1939, when she emerged in S&M olive green livery, the only one to bear a new number. No. 8182 was photographed in May 1932. (H.C.Casserley)

RAILCARS

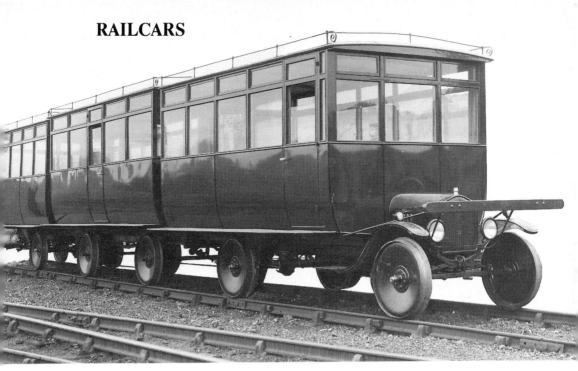

14. In an attempt to reduce operating costs, Colonel Stephens introduced petrol railcars, which unfortunately acted as a deterrent to passengers on account of their noise and vibration. The bodies were constructed by Edmunds of Thetford in 1923 on Ford chassis, built in the USA under licence. As the set was only ever driven by one axle, the centre car could not be used on the S&M gradients. (D.Churchill coll.)

→

15. Col. Stephens' prototype railcar was a single vehicle with a custom built body on a Wolseley - Siddeley chassis of 1908 vintage. It ran trials on the Kent & East Sussex, and was transferred to the West Sussex Railway where it formed half of a hybrid passenger/goods set in the company of a converted Ford lorry. In this form it was transferred again, this time to the Shropshire and Montgomeryshire. The engine had been damaged beyond repair before leaving the WSR, so it never ran under its own power on the S&M. (Lens of Sutton)

16. In 1937 the body from the Wolseley - Siddeley railcar was mounted on the ex-LCC horse tram chassis to form a trailer for *Gazelle*. After closure the body survived as a shed at Kinnerley, where it was photographed in 1958. It was acquired for preservation in 1986 and completely dismantled. (H.C.Casserley)

LLANYMYNECH

The 1887 map shows the Cambrian Railway's Welshpool - Oswestry line from left to right and the Llanfyllin branch, along with the Shropshire Union Canal, top right. The double track connection to the "Potts" is on the left - the single connection, nearer to their turntable and locomotive shed, was not restored by Stephens. The shed was destroyed by fire on 29th October 1937.

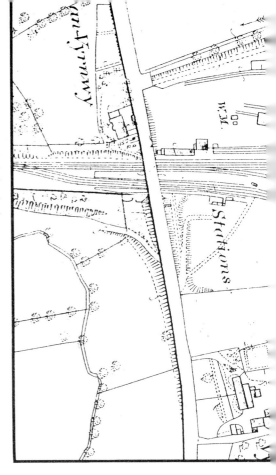

SHROPSHIRE & MONTGOMERYSHIRE RLY.

FORD & CROSSGATES
TO
LLANYMYNECH   JCT.

1st CLASS.   Fare 18

LLANYMYNECH JCT.   LLANYMYNECH JCT.

0468

17. "The Potts" had one of its two locomotive sheds at Llanymynech but Stephens decided that a single shed at Kinnerley would be better. The disused shed is seen to the left of the ex-MR coaches, which are hauled by 0-6-2T no. 6 *Thisbe*. (L.Darbyshire coll.)

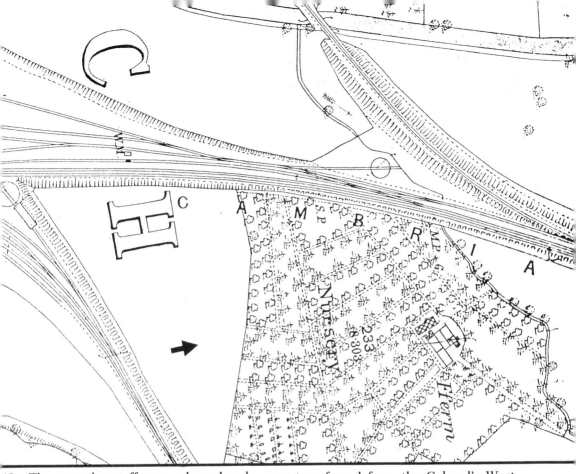

18. The operating staff were ashamed and apologetic when passengers approached the "train", the noise and vibration having no passenger appeal whatsoever. The Ford lorry was transferred from the Colonel's West Sussex Railway and is seen coupled to a Ford railcar in about 1926.
(Col. Stephens Railway Archives)

19. Many writers have ridiculed the sign on the right, suggesting that there were *quicker* railway routes, but the alternatives involved changes at Buttington or Wittington and much greater journey times. No. 8182 is seen passing the steel-legged water tower on 28th May 1932.

The temporary wooden structure seen in picture no. 17 had been erected owing to its predecessor having been consumed by fire allegedly started by a spark from a Cambrian engine. (H.C.Casserley)

21. On the right, wagons stand on the former connecting line, while cattle wagons are in profusion in the GWR yard. Ex-Cambrian Railways 0-6-0 no. 893 is bound for Welshpool on 5th August 1935.
(R.K.Cope/R.S.Carpenter)

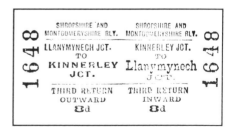

| 1648 | SHROPSHIRE AND MONTGOMERYSHIRE RLY.
LLANYMYNECH JCT.
TO
KINNERLEY JCT.
THIRD RETURN
OUTWARD
8d | SHROPSHIRE AND MONTGOMERYSHIRE RLY.
KINNERLEY JCT.
TO
Llanymynech JCT.
THIRD RETURN
INWARD
8d | 1648 |

20. Another 1932 photograph records some manual activity on the weed adorned S&M tracks, while an ex-Cambrian Railway 4-4-0, no. 1043, runs in from Oswestry. Note the dropped joint (bent rail end) lower right.
(S.W.Baker)

22.   After cessation of regular passenger services, no. 1 *Gazelle* was available for hire by private parties, the group being carried in a railcar body, mounted on the tramcar chassis, which had been shortened by over 3ft. and fitted with buffers.   BLC refers to the Birmingham Locomotive Club which travelled the line on 23rd April 1939 and which was one of the last organisations to use this unusual combination. (R.K.Cope/R.S.Carpenter)

23.   A 1954 view shows the original "Potts" building on the left and the junction signal box in the distance. The WD relaid most of the track with flat bottom rail, an example of which is seen on the left. (J.J.Smith)

24. WD 0-6-0ST no. 188 was recorded on 21st September 1958, passing the sign that deterred many railway enthusiasts. The Army continued to operate public goods traffic on the line until 29th February 1960. (H.C.Casserley)

25. An SLS special stands on relaid track on 21st September 1958. The "water tank" appears to have been formed from four separate tanks. No. 188 was built by the Vulcan Foundry in 1945. (H.C.Casserley)

26. Industrial premises near completion by the S&M trackbed as BR class 4 2-6- 4T no. 80096 arrives from Oswestry on 24th October 1964. The former GWR goods yard closed on 6th July 1964 and passenger services ceased on 18th January 1965. (E.Wilmshurst)

27. Seen on the same day, the signal box then controlled only a short siding on the former S&M route. The earlier double connection was reputedly unique on British light railways. The raised part of the platform was to facilitate the unloading and loading of cattle and milk churns. (E.Wilmshurst)

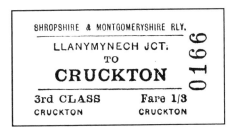

28. Looking back towards the station in 1937, we see the signals for the two platforms. Lack of interlocking equipment allowed the right signal to be off while the points are set to the left! (R.K.Cope/R.S.Carpenter)

29. Looking west, one mile from Llanymynech, we see the substantial bridge carrying the B4398 to Knockin. Its dimensions are a reminder that the route was laid with double track as part of an intended main line. (R.K.Cope/R.S.Carpenter)

MAESBROOK

30. The house and station were erected by the PS&NWR but the square board with diagonal line was erected by the S&M. It could be rotated by passengers wishing to stop the train and is seen in 1931.
(R.K.Cope/R.S.Carpenter)

The 1902 edition marks a weighing machine (W.M.), which had a capacity of seven tons. Three additional sidings were laid in 1941. The main traffic was coal inwards and sugar beet outwards. In the severe floods of 1947, a small bridge, east of the station, was destroyed.

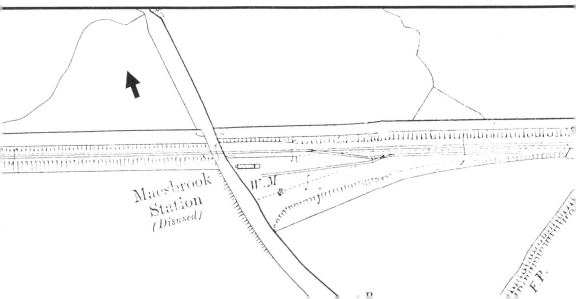

Maesbrook
Station
(Disused)

W.M

31. The SLS railtour stops for enthusiasts to examine the station from every viewpoint, including the train roof. Details of the WD version of the stop board are evident in this photograph taken on 21st September 1958. (J.J.Smith)

32. Llanymynech Hill is in the background of this 1958 picture, which shows variation in platform level. The house still stands although much modernised and extended. During WWII, the crossing was fitted with the now familiar lifting barriers, but then rare and hand operated. (R.M.Casserley)

WERN LAS

Notice of siding opening dated July 1926.

33. A 1937 eastward view shows the crossing cottage built by "The Potts" and the platform, lamp and seat added by the "Colonel" in 1911. The cottage was still occupied in 1990. (S.W.Baker)

34. Looking west in 1958, only the track appears to have improved. The halt was situated at the meeting point of four minor roads but the population of the area was very sparse. (R.M.Casserley)

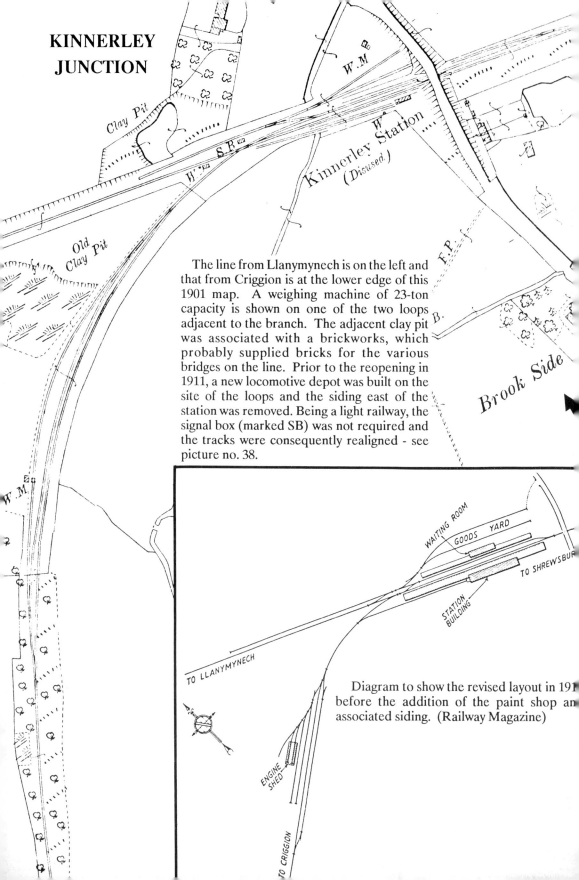

KINNERLEY JUNCTION

Clay Pit

W.M.

W. S.B.

Kinnerley Station
(Disused)

Old Clay Pit

F.P.

B.

Brook Side

The line from Llanymynech is on the left and that from Criggion is at the lower edge of this 1901 map. A weighing machine of 23-ton capacity is shown on one of the two loops adjacent to the branch. The adjacent clay pit was associated with a brickworks, which probably supplied bricks for the various bridges on the line. Prior to the reopening in 1911, a new locomotive depot was built on the site of the loops and the siding east of the station was removed. Being a light railway, the signal box (marked SB) was not required and the tracks were consequently realigned - see picture no. 38.

W.M.

WAITING ROOM

GOODS YARD

TO SHREWSBUR

STATION BUILDING

TO LLANYMYNECH

ENGINE SHED

TO CRIGGION

Diagram to show the revised layout in 191 before the addition of the paint shop an associated siding. (Railway Magazine)

35. Local residents must have thought that wonders never cease when the first train arrived for over twenty years. The siding does not yet have buffers and the ground frame (left) is devoid of a shelter, but no doubt the gathered company were duly impressed. Stephens appears to be walking towards the camera. (Colonel Stephens Railway Archives)

36. The locomotive of the 2pm from Shrewsbury on 18th July 1919 had just been changed to no. 5, an ex-LSWR "Ilfracombe Goods" built in 1874 and purchased for the S&M in 1914. Kinnerley had a population of slightly over 1000 during the life of the S&M. (K.Nunn/LCGB)

37. Barrels and churns wait by the goods shed, which does not appear in the reopening photograph. The diminutive 0-4-2T *Gazelle* worked the Criggion branch for many years and is seen here on 28th August 1926, at which time there were two return journeys on weekdays on the branch. (H.C.Casserley)

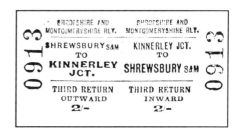

	SHROPSHIRE AND MONTGOMERYSHIRE RLY.	SHROPSHIRE AND MONTGOMERYSHIRE RLY.	
0913	SHREWSBURY S&M TO **KINNERLEY JCT.**	KINNERLEY JCT. TO SHREWSBURY S&M	0913
	THIRD RETURN OUTWARD 2/-	THIRD RETURN INWARD 2/-	

38. A mixed train waits in the down platform for a locomotive to emerge from the shed, top left, the operation being controlled from the ground frame under the shelter at the end of the up platform. This had 13 levers, one of which was spare. The timbered part of the platforms were used for the handling of milk churns. (Col. Stephens Railway Archives)

39. A railcar stands beyond the ground frame, while other stock is berthed on the main line. The bay platform was intended for the Criggion branch train but invariably accommodated idle, crippled or life expired vehicles. (Lens of Sutton)

40. A small crowd has gathered for the excursion on August Bank Holiday Monday, 1935. Note the buttoned upholstery on the coach doors, also the economical way that Stephens raised the level of the up platform, and finally the railcar radiator contemptuously discarded by the ground frame. Single line safety was ensured by electric train tablet to Ford, staff and ticket to Llanymynech and one engine in steam to Criggion. (H.F.Wheeller)

41. A few minutes later, the excursion arrived from Shrewsbury, behind no. 8236. Within a few seconds of it leaving for Llanymynech, no. 8108 departed from the bay platform, bound for Criggion with a van and two four-wheelers. On the right is one of a number of wooden bungalows erected for staff use and still standing in 1990. (H.F.Wheeller)

42. Earlier that day, excursionists from the morning train from Shrewsbury found that they had to cross to the up platform to travel in a dilapidated railcar to Criggion. The bay platform was already occupied by empty coaches. (H.F.Wheeller)

43. The line continued to carry substantial quantities of local merchandise throughout the war but, by 1947, this was the only notice of the service. The Colonel had earlier spent £16 on a motor cycle for his station agent to use to visit potential customers. A donkey cart was in use from 1929-38, for local deliveries and collections. (H.C.Casserley)

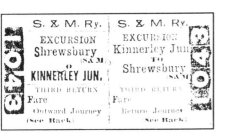

45. Two vehicles from the LSWR's royal train were acquired by Stephens. Built in the 1840s, one went to the K&ESR and the other survived on the S&M to become personnel carrier in the Army's breakdown train, being visible next to the brake van in the previous picture. It is seen here in 1935, in use on an excursion train. (H.F.Wheeller)

44. A 1958 view makes interesting comparison with picture no. 38 as it shows that the Army rearranged the track and signalling, additionally providing a new signal box and reconditioning the locomotive shed. The original "Potts" building remained on the down platform. (J.J.Smith)

SHROPSHIRE AND MONTGOMERY-SHIRE RAILWAY		
Composite Rate (Standard Rate plus 28s. War Advance)		

GRADE.		
	s.	d.
Station Agent—		
Shrewsbury	109	0
Ford and Crossgate...	†93	6
Nesscliffe	97	6
Kinnerley	103	6
Clerk—		
Shrewsbury	89	6
Guard	92	6
Porter	82	0
Ganger	88	6
Lengthman	82	0
Driver	111	6

	Base Rate.		War Adv'nce	
	s.	d.	s.	d.
Fitter-in-Charge	*69	0	31	0
Assistant Fitter	50	0	36	0
Carpenter	61	0	35	6

NOTE
* Special rate to holder of position at November, 1945.
† To be increased to 97s. 6d. after 12 months' service in position.

46. Although chaired track was retained between the platforms and in some sidings, the WD relaid the junction with heavy flat-bottom rail. The van on the right is endorsed **BREAKDOWN TRAIN.**
(R.K.Cope/R.S.Carpenter)

48. Continuing the Colonel's tradition of providing unusual rolling stock, eight ex-London, Tilbury & Southend Railway coaches were provided by the WD, these having once worked the Ealing-Southend service along the District Line. The Army also ran four ex-GWR clerestory bogie coaches.
(H.C.Casserley)

47. The railtour on 14th September 1958 stopped at the junction for photographic purposes. The record includes some of the numerous Nissen huts and the lattice signal post that replaced the earlier wooden one. The previous bracket signal had been blown off at the end of 1938. (S.C.Nash)

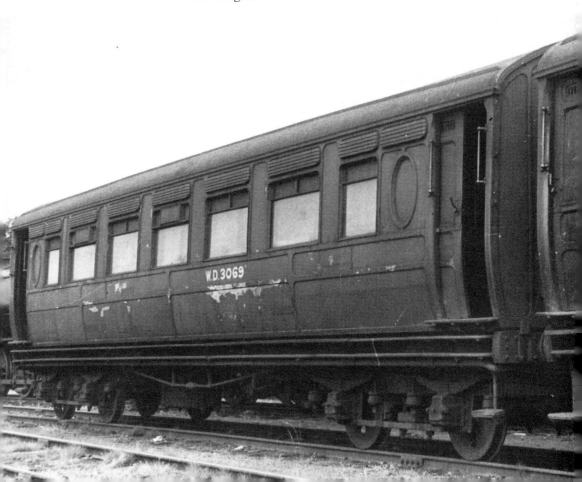

KINNERLEY SHED

49. The timber framed shed was erected in 1910 on the wide strip of land earlier used for sidings by the PS&NWR. The lean-to part of the building housed the machine shop, seen in the next illustration. The sheds and staff cottages were similar to those erected by Stephens at Rolvenden - see our *Branch Line to Tenterden*.
(Colonel Stephens Railway Archives)

50. A 1941 inventory is summarised as follows: Cochran vertical boiler - flue pitted and safety valve sticks. Vernon & Guest 6ft lathe - driving gears worn and traversing track loose, with some teeth missing. Planing machine - traversing pinion broken. Steam hammer - disconnected and rusted up. Grindstone - runs off centre by 1". Forge - back plate patched and tuyere burst. Horizontal engine - knock in gudgeon pin and regulator unusable (steam shut off at boiler). Worthington force pump - shoulder of stock broken off. Blake & Coy force pump - serviceable but water spindle worn. Bipolar dynamo - out of use. Shafting - pulley blocks worn and belts unreliable.
(Colonel Stephens Railway Archives).

51. A northward view in August 1935, includes the wheels of *Dido*, an S&M cattle truck, the tank of *Dido*, coaches 8 and 12, a 3-plank wagon and no. 6 *Thisby*. On the left is the paint shop, the brick building probably being the PS&NWR weighhouse, marked on the 1901 map. (H.F.Wheeller)

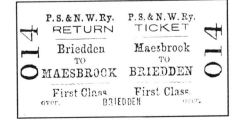

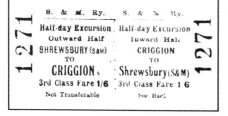

52. No. 8108 was purchased from the LMS in March 1930, over a year before the Colonel's death, but shortly after he had suffered a debilitating stroke. The windpump in the background was one of his ideas for economical operation of light railways. Similar means of raising water from a well to the tank were found on most of his other lines. Near the decaying shed on 5th August 1935 is "Ilfracombe Goods" no. 3 *Hesperus*. (H.F.Wheeller)

54. South of the locomotive shed was the paint shop, identifiable by the patches left on the door from brush cleaning activities. No. 1 and the S&M's equivalent of a land cruise train is seen in about 1937, along with the branch junction signals. (Lens of Sutton)

53. In this southward view from June 1932, the Criggion branch is to the left of ex-LBSCR Terrier no. 9 *Daphne*. This engine was purchased from the War Stores Disposal Board in 1923 and sold to the SR in 1938 for spares. On the left is the loop for stone trains. (S.W.Baker)

55. The WD refurbished the shed in July 1941 but retained the old coal dock and water tank, as seen in June 1947. "Dean Goods" no. 180 was built as no.2514 by the GWR in 1898 and had the Westinghouse air pump bracket fitted by the Army. (H.C.Casserley)

56. The winter of 1947 was exceptionally severe and caused great difficulty for railway operators. Frost and snow are evident, but it was only 3rd September. Centre is Avonside 0-6-0ST *Ashford*, built in 1920 and used by the Army from 1942 until 1949. (S.W.Baker)

57. By 1958, the WD had erected a new and higher water tower, with a supplementary one by the coal dock, clearer in the next picture. The Nissen hut, on the left, was used for housing the Wickham and Drewry petrol railcars. (H.C.Casserley)

58. Another 1958 view reveals details such as the ash pit and the water tank brazier for use in times of frost. Nos. 141 and 143 were standard WD Austerity 0-6-0STs, built in 1944, and were typical of the 19 similar engines used on the line during the latter part of the period of Government requisition. (S.C.Nash)

CRIGGION BRANCH
CHAPEL LANE

59. The halt served about 24 dwellings in the Crosslanes and Melverley Green area and first appeared in the timetables in 1921, but was always shown as a request stop. Viewed towards Kinnerley in 1949, the siding remained available for agricultural traffic until that year. It was situated one mile south of the junction, but no chapel existed in the lane at that time. (R.K.Cope/R.S.Carpenter)

MELVERLEY

60. No reason has been found for the provision of this expensive seven-arch bridge to carry a quiet lane which only had a level crossing over the busier line at Nesscliff & Pentre. A light engine, an "Ilfracombe Goods", is proceeding towards Criggion. (Colonel Stephens Railway Archives)

← The 1882 survey shows that the only dwelling nearby was that of the rector, who had under 200 parishioners.

61. During the visit of the Stephenson Locomotive Society to the S&M on 14th September 1958, an excursion on the branch was arranged, using two Drewry petrol railcars. The bridge was subsequently demolished, leaving the lane on a slight embankment to this day. (J.J.Smith)

62. In 1902, during the period of dormancy of the line, Melverley Viaduct was destroyed by the raging River Severn. Here we witness reconstruction in progress in 1912. (Col. Stephens Railway Archives)

64. In 1947, the GWR designed a new bridge, which was built by A.E.Farr Ltd in the following year. In 1962, the bridge was adapted to carry a road and it continues to serve this useful purpose to this day, providing an additional link between England and Wales. (R.K.Cope/R.S.Carpenter)

63. In 1932, the structure was considered unfit for passengers and so services, minimal as they were, terminated at Melverley. £280 was spent on repairs but problems recurred on 27th January 1940, when ice flows carried away six piles and some bracing, isolating 64 wagons. Repairs were completed by 27th October 1941 but by 1945 the integrity of the structure was in such doubt that only the quarry's Sentinel shunter was allowed to pass over it with the stone trains. (Col. Stephens Railway Archives)

CREW GREEN

65. The first station on the route to be situated in Montgomeryshire, it was equipped with a tramcar seat, from the LCC vehicle brought by Mr. Stephens for use on the branch. Its back could be repositioned, according to the direction of travel. This is a view towards Melverley in 1937. (R.K.Cope/R.S.Carpenter)

66. Beyond the three wagons are five 15ft diameter iron huts. Eight of these ex-Army structures were purchased in 1927 by the enterprising Colonel and let out for camping purposes, at 7/- per week. There were two at Shrawardine and one at Criggion. The company also hired out two skiffs and two dinghies at 6d per hour. Other views of the round huts can be found in our *East Kent Light Railways,* pictures 21 and 117. (R.K.Cope/R.S.Carpenter)

LLANDRINIO ROAD

67. Breidden Hill is in the background of this 1950 view, which includes stone wagons in the solitary siding. Note the serious defects in the brickwork of the cottage and the buttress added to treat it. (G.Bannister)

68. When photographed in 1958, little had changed, apart from the loss of the crossing cottage. Other than one farm, there were no dwellings in the locality but nevertheless the station was a mandatory stop for passenger trains. The population of the parish was about 700 but the village was two miles to the west. (H.C.Casserley)

NORTH OF CRIGGION

69. On August Bank Holiday Monday of 1935, the driver of the excursion had to lock the catch points before proceeding towards Criggion loop. He is returning to his "train", a pair of Ford railcars. (H.F.Wheeller)

P. S. & N. W. Ry
MAESBROOK to
BRIEDDEN
PARLIAMENTARY.
This Ticket is issued subject to the con
ditions stated on the Co's. Time Bills.
BRIEDDEN

041

S. & M. Ry.
EXCURSION
LLANDRINIO ROAD
TO
SHREWSBURY
THIRD RETURN
Fare **2**s. **8**d.
Inward Journey
(SEE BACK)

S. & M. Ry.
EXCURSION
SHREWSBURY
TO
Llandrinio Road
THIRD RETURN
Fare **2**s. **8**d.
Outward Journey
(SEE BACK)

0077

0077

CRIGGION

70. Passengers on the morning excursion from Shrewsbury on 5th August 1935 were conveyed by Ford railcars to Criggion, arriving at about noon. "The Rattlers" are about to return empty, leaving their passengers with a ringing noise in their ears from the din created by the pressed steel wheels. This was the penultimate year of railcar operation. (H.F.Wheeller)

71. On 23rd April 1939, the Birmingham Locomotive Club included the branch in its itinery. *Gazelle* and its unique coach have just passed the loop siding. As this was occupied, the coach was presumably propelled back to the junction. (R.K.Cope/R.S.Carpenter)

72. The British Quarry Company's Sentinel shunter propels loaded wagons towards the station (right) on 21st April 1950. The vicar of the church in the background wrote a letter to the Board of Trade complaining that he was forced to ride on an engine (*Gazelle*), as no coach was provided. With less than 120 parishioners, he had adequate time to dwell upon such distress for which a high price would later be paid. (G.Bannister)

Criggion Vicarage,
Shrewsbury.

23rd November 1912

Sir,
  I booked today my fare by the 3.57 train from Abbey Gate station to Criggion on the Shropshire & Montgomery Rly.
  I rode to Kinnerley Junction by a properly equipped train.
  Proceeding by the branch to Criggion, I was put with another man and two women into the back part of an engine with only a screen between us and the fire - no roof, and the sparks and smuts falling all over us - one spark nearly got into my eye - with danger of being blinded - my clothes too injured by the same.
  I wish to know whether passengers can be thus treated and deceived - for the last train I caught about a fortnight ago I was incarcerated in a carriage as I have hitherto been.
  I have had occasion to use the railway for my wife and daughters and friends from London, and of course I cannot subject them to such risk & barbarous treatment.
  If they cannot or will not serve proper accommodation through the journey, they should not be allowed to advertise it - there were carriages at the Station (Kinnerley), and as an engine ran - a carriage could and should have been on the back.
  Another matter of which I have complained, and which the Supt. has promised to have remedied is the hollow appropriately termed a ditch by one of the officials, formed by sinking the rails, or making proper approaches to the crossing to my church - trusting that these matters may be inquired into and remedied.
  I am your obedient servant,

R. Brock

Vicar of Criggion

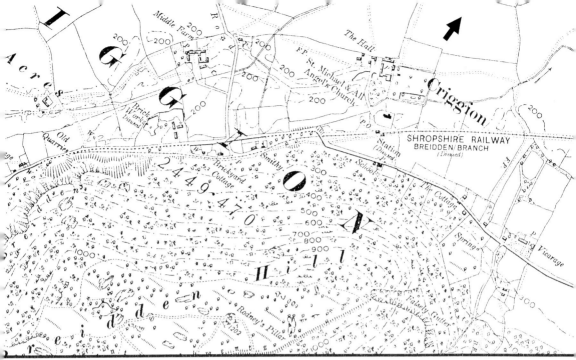

The 1902 edition at 6" to 1 mile shows *disused* brickworks, *disused* station and *old* quarries - a depressed area indeed. The revival of the railway in 1912 must have brought new hope for the villagers.

73. Owing to its popularity, the SLS railtour, seen at Melverley, was repeated a week later, by which time the engine cover of no. 9105 had been replaced. The residents of Criggion parish had been adequately served by buses since the mid-1920s. (H.C.Casserley)

CRIGGION QUARRY

74. The train in picture no. 72 is seen earlier on its journey between the quarry and the station. The dome accommodated the two vertical cylinders, while the vertical boiler was situated in the cab. In 1928-29, Sentinel Wagon Works (1920) Ltd used the S&M to test run some new locomotives, the line being reasonably close to their Shrewsbury works. (G.Bannister)

75. The processing plant and loading facility is seen on 21st September 1958, on the occasion of the SLS visit. The Greenstone of the Breidden Hill is Dolerite, but has often been wrongly described as Granite. (H.C.Casserley)

76. Looking in the other direction on the same day, the neglected trackwork and small locomotive shed are visible. The short chimney of the 1927 Sentinel is also evident.

The cessation of stone traffic to S&M stations in 1939 was due to local road transport being more economical by then. (J.J.Smith)

Year	To intermediate stations on the S.& M.Rly. tons	To main line companies. tons	TOTAL tons
Jan.-Dec.			
1935	5196	34990	40186
1936	3738	18747	22485
1937	2788	16143	18931
1938	3467	13469	17116
1939	Nil	15000	15000
1940	During this period all stone was conveyed by road to		
1941	Four Crosses Station, Melverley Bridge being unserviceable.		
Nov-Oct.			
1942-3	Nil	22540	22540
1943-4	Nil	24920	24920
1944-5	Nil	22856	22856
1945-6	Nil	20246	20246
1946-7	Nil	20536	20536
1947-8	Nil	21169	21169

EDGERLEY

SHROPSHIRE & MONTGOMERYSHIRE RLY.

NESSCLIFFE

TO

SHREWSBURY S. & M.

THIRD CLASS   Fare 1/9
Shrewsbury S.& M.   Shrewsbury S.& M.

8130

77. The platform was brought into use in 1927 and photographed ten years later. Access was from the south, via a footpath through the woods on the left. It was near Turfmoor but was not marked on the 1" Ordnance Survey. (R.K.Cope/R.S.Carpenter)

SHROPSHIRE & MONTGOMERYSHIRE RLY.

NESSCLIFF

TO

FORD & CROSSGATES

3rd CLASS   Fare 6d.
FORD & CROSSGATES   FORD & CROSSGATES

1572   1572

SHROPSHIRE AND MONTGOMERYSHIRE RLY.	SHROPSHIRE AND MONTGOMERYSHIRE RLY.
NESCLIFFE	MAESBROOK
TO	TO
MAESBROOK	NESCLIFFE
THIRD RETURN OUTWARD 8D.	THIRD RETURN INWARD 8D.

0219   0219

NESSCLIFF & PENTRE

78. By 1935, most of the line was heavily overgrown but here the track was fairly clear. Ladies laze on the well cut grass, as the August Bank Holiday excursion leaves. An old five-compartment coach body serves as a store near the goods loop. (H.F.Wheeller)

The 1882 survey marks the loop and two sidings which were retained during the 1910 relaying.

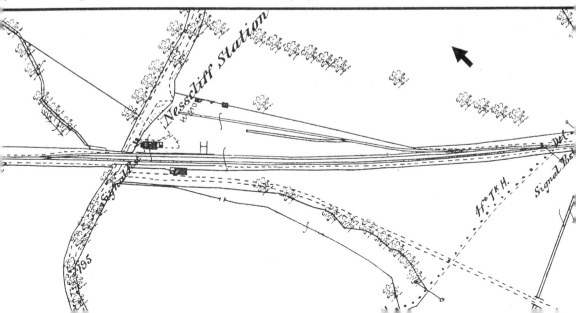

79. Opened by the "Potts", the station was a scheduled stop for most trains. WD no. 75187 is seen with the S&M daily goods train to Llanymynech in April 1947. (G.F.Bannister)

80. A westward view in 1958 shows the Army's lifting barriers in a vertical position and also the original crossing cottage. It appears that the pre-war goods loop had been retained (R.M.Casserley)

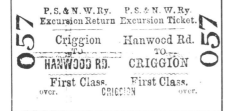

P.S.& N.W.Ry.	P.S.& N.W.Ry.
Excursion Return	Excursion Ticket.
Criggion	Hanwood Rd.
TO	TO
HANWOOD RD.	CRIGGION
First Class.	First Class.
over.	CRIGGION	over.

81. Pentre Halt was built by the Army south-east of Nesscliff and Pentre. Nearby a branch northwards terminated in a four-platformed terminus at Nesscliff Camp, the station being known unofficially as "Lonsdale". This is the view towards Kinnerley in 1958. (R.M.Casserley)

SHRAWARDINE

82. A new building was erected in 1910, along with a rotatable stop board and lamp, for use by the 179 parishioners when required. The cattle grid was required on light railways where no level crossing gates were provided. (Colonel Stephens Railway Archives)

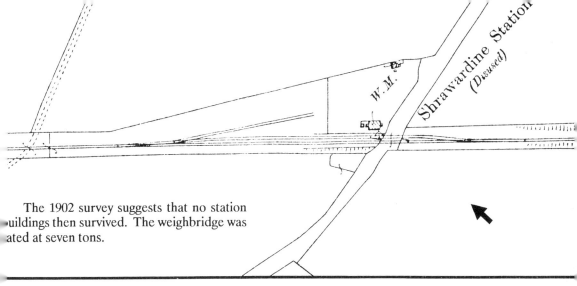

W.M.

Shrawardine Station *(Disused)*

The 1902 survey suggests that no station
buildings then survived. The weighbridge was
rated at seven tons.

83. An eastward view in 1935 shows part of the
former up platform, used in the early days of
the PS&NWR when double track was in use.
A few passengers have just alighted from the
August Bank Holiday excursion.
(H.F.Wheeller)

84. A 1958 picture reveals that the Army laid
a considerable length of double track and also
provided extra sidings and a water tank. The
original crossing cottage survived, although it
had been gutted by fire on 1st November 1941.
(R.M.Casserley)

85. A 1910 view of the massive viaduct includes the contractor's 0-6-0ST, built by Manning Wardle. At this time, the only connection to other railways was at Llanymynech.
(Colonel Stephens Railway Archives)

86. A potentially catastrophic derailment took place when 0-6-2T *Thisbe* broke a pony truck spring, in about 1914.
(Colonel Stephens Railway Archives)

87. This view towards Kinnerley in 1937 shows the curve of the bridge. Stability of the columns was a serious problem that resulted in the Royal Engineers erecting new spans on the disused abutments in 1947. The increased permitted axle load resulted in the introduction of the WD "Austerity" 0-6-0STs.
(R.K.Cope/R.S.Carpenter)

No. 193 hauls the BLC Special over the new bridge in June 1955. The structure was dismantled in April 1962. (G.F.Bannister)

FORD AND CROSSGATES

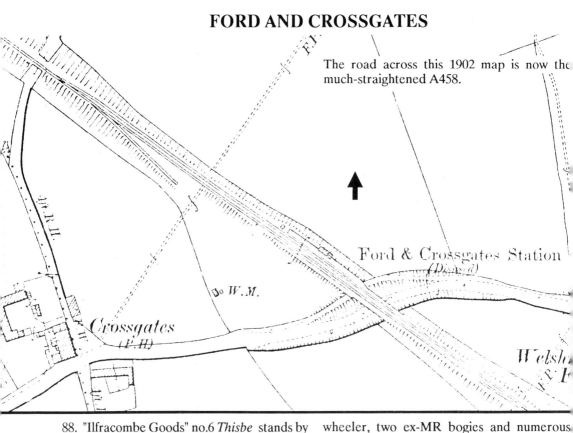

The road across this 1902 map is now the much-straightened A458.

88. "Ilfracombe Goods" no.6 *Thisbe* stands by one of the PS&NWR buildings with the 9.45am Shrewsbury to Llanymynech on 18th July 1919. The train is composed of an ex-LSWR four wheeler, two ex-MR bogies and numerous wagons. It was the frequent shunting of mixed trains of this type that caused passengers so much discomfort and stress. (K.Nunn/LCGB)

89. Ex-LNWR "Collier" no. 8182 heads north with an ex-MR van loaded with parcels, followed by mixed freight, on 2nd September 1937. Only one trip a day was made at this time. The combined populations of the two villages rose from 320 to 380 during the period 1911 to 1931. (R.K.Cope/R.S.Carpenter)

90. A northward view in 1938 gives details of the road bridge, which was demolished after closure, only the northern abutment now being visible. When photographed in 1938, the down line (left) was seldom used. (R.K.Cope/R.S.Carpenter)

91. Looking towards Shrewsbury from an excursion on 5th August 1935, we see the unimposing exit. The path turned left, down to the main road. A similar path was provided from the other platform - hence the foot crossing. (H.F.Wheeller)

92. A few minutes later, the north end of the loop, the disused down signal and the entrance to the goods yard came into view. Staff and ticket single line operation was in force to Shrewsbury, while electric tablet was used to Kinnerley. The ground frame (just out of view, on the left) had seven levers, one of which was spare. (R.K.Cope/R.S.Carpenter)

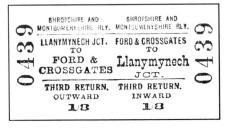

93. A 1958 view towards Kinnerley shows that the Army had doubled much of the track in this area. An inventory in 1941 listed one bench (used as a desk), one tow rope (broken), one trolley (porters), four seats (platform), two handlamps (one serviceable), one generator (acetylene) and four notice boards - LNWR, S&M, LMS and LBSCR. (R.M.Casserley)

SHOOT HILL

94. The Army retained the original stone platform facing and added a hut for the benefit of the operator of the barriers. When photographed in 1958, this type of crossing protection was still regarded as "continental". (R.M.Casserley)

CRUCKTON

95. Cruckton was one of the new stops opened by the S&M and had an all brick platform edge, the earlier stations being largely constructed in stone. This was always shown as a request stop, as there were few houses in the vicinity. (R.K.Cope/R.S.Carpenter)

Shropshire & Montgomeryshire Rly.

CHEAP
EXCURSION TRAIN

Will run from SHREWSBURY (Abbey Station) every THURSDAY, until further notice, to the following Stations, at the fares shewn below, to

LLANYMYNECH

For LAKE VYRNWY, Etc.

AND

Criggion (for the Breidden Hills), Etc.

BEAUTIFUL SCENERY.   CHARMING WALKS.

On Thursday September 16th and three following Thursdays Sept. 23rd, 30th, and October 7th a MOTOR will run from LLANYMYNECH to LAKE VYRNWY after the arrival of the 9-45 a.m. train from Shrewsbury, and return from the Lake to connect with the 5-10 p.m. train from Llanymynech to Shrewsbury. Fare for the double journey, 6/6 each passenger, in addition to railway fare Shrewsbury to Llanymynech.

Depart Shrewsbury for Llanymynech,
9-45 a.m. & 2 p.m.

Depart Shrewsbury for Criggion,
9-45 a.m.

Fare, Third Class:

3/1½

Available for return from Llanymynech 5-10 p.m. same day.
„   „   Criggion   4-45 p.m.   „

Tickets issued to Criggion will be available for return from Llanymynech.
Teas and Refreshments can be obtained at the Lake Vyrnwy Hotel.

For Handbills and all further information, apply to
Mr. J. L. WHITE, Abbey Station ;

EDGEBOLD

96.   A 1931 eastward view suggests that spot resleepering had recently taken place, using untreated timber - a proven false economy. The poles carry an unusual number of insulators - presumably the GPO had a wayleave for a pole route in this area. A siding for a dairy was in use from 1942 and removed in 1954. (R.K.Cope/R.S.Carpenter)

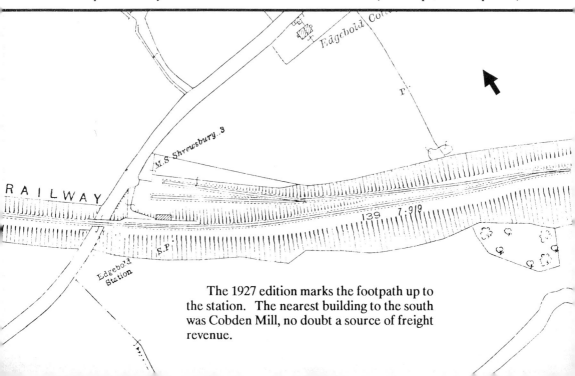

The 1927 edition marks the footpath up to the station. The nearest building to the south was Cobden Mill, no doubt a source of freight revenue.

97.   The bridge over the A458 is seen from the west end of Edgebold platform in October 1931.   The stopping place was one of those added in 1911 and was listed as Hanwood Road until 1920, it becoming a request stop for most trains thereafter.
(R.K.Cope/R.S.Carpenter)

98.   Half a mile south-east of Edgebold station, the route crossed over the LMS & GWR joint line between Shrewsbury and Welshpool.   Passengers on this route can still see the brick abutments clearly.
(R.M.Casserley)

HOOKAGATE

99. The S&M ran roughly parallel to the LMS/GWR route for about three miles. Both are seen in 1935, by which time the stop board was redundant. The station was known as Redhill until 1920 and by 1925 most trains were shown as stopping only upon request. (H.F.Wheeller)

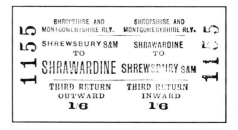

100. A 1937 westward view from the platform shows the limited extent of the goods yard. The PS&NWR Redhill station had been near the far end of the yard. (R.K.Cope/R.S.Carpenter)

101. Hookagate station was still complete when recorded in August 1937 but it was destroyed in 1941, when the WD established extensive exchange sidings with the main line in this area. (R.K.Cope/R.S.Carpenter)

102. The cutting was widened considerably and nine tracks laid south of the S&M main line on which a troop train is running behind no. 70196. The locomotives awaiting the breakers on 1st April 1947 were nos. 70095, 8182, 8108 and 8236. In the foreground is no. 70093. (J.G.Vincent)

04. At the Shrewsbury end of the site, there was a connection with the main line, which passed under the long span of the road bridge, seen in 1949. The Army used lower quadrant signals here in order that there was consistency with adjacent GWR ones. Elsewhere on the S&M, upper quadrants were installed. In 1959, BR built a rail welding plant on the site, which remained in use until May 1986, the signal box having closed in November 1973. (R.K.Cope/R.S.Carpenter)

103. Looking towards Shrewsbury on 23rd July 1948, the back row includes 70096, 70197, 70094, 70095, 8182, 8108 and 8236, while in the near row there are nos. 70169, 70196 and 70175. In the background is the bridge seen in picture no. 99. (J.J.Smith)

MEOLE BRACE

105. This was another station added by Stephens in 1911 and was one of the better patronised stops as the area was effectively a suburb of Shrewsbury. All trains were time-tabled to call here and tickets were collected during the stop. The single siding, used mainly for domestic coal, is beyond the platform in this 1958 picture. (H.C.Casserley)

The 1927 edition shows the Meole Brace exchange sidings laid down by Stephens in 1910. The "Potts" had connections at Llanymynech and east of Shrewsbury, on the Wellington line.

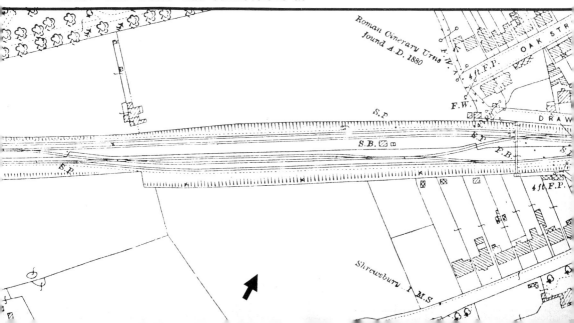

EAST OF MEOLE BRACE

106. "Collier" no. 8182 approaches Meole Brace with the "daily" goods on 2nd September 1937. The guard travelled with the parcels in the leading van, the lack of a brake van facilitating shunting at intermediate stations. (R.K.Cope/R.S.Carpenter)

107. The exchange sidings were of insufficient capacity for the WD - hence the provision of more extensive facilities at Hookagate. The Army was not empowered to lift the S&M sidings and so they were still present in 1949, although disconnected. (The requisition order only covered Llanymynech to Hookagate.) This view dates from October 1931 and includes Meole Brace Junction signal box. (R.K.Cope/R.S.Carpenter)

108. The previous picture was taken from this footbridge, which, although rebuilt, was still in use in 1990. The tidiness of the track suggests that this photograph might have been taken at the time of reopening.
(Colonel Stephens Railway Archives)

109. This 1937 photograph shows the relationship of the footbridge to the "halt" at Shrewsbury West, which was situated under the roadbridge. Trains to and from Shrewsbury General used the arch on the left
(R.K.Cope/R.S.Carpenter)

Shropshire & Montgomeryshire Railway.

GOLF
AT
LLANYMYNECH

RETURN THIRD CLASS TICKETS will be issued daily (Sundays excepted) commencing **JULY 25th, 1921,** and until further notice, by the Trains and Stations shewn below, on presentation of Golf Club Membership Tickets or Vouchers, obtainable from Golf Club.

	FARES.	
SHREWSBURY	3/8	
MEOLE BRACE	3/6	Available by 9-45 a.m.
HOOKAGATE	3/3	daily and 2 p.m. trains
EDGEBOLD	2/11	ex Shrewsbury. (3 p.m.
FORD and		Wednesdays).
CROSSGATES	2/5	

Available to return from Llanymynech by 5-25 p.m. train daily and Saturdays only 8-10 p.m.

ABBEY STATION, SHREWSBURY.
April, 1921.

H. F. STEPHENS, Managing Director.

Livesey Ltd., Printers, St. John's Hill, Shrewsbury.

SHREWSBURY WEST

110. Being located under the A49 bridge, no other shelter was provided for passengers. The infrequency of trains and the remoteness of the terminus from the town centre combined to produce poor passenger figures here. This part of the bridge was eliminated soon after closure, to improve the road alignment. The halt was known unofficially as "Belle Vue Platform".

(Colonel Stephens Railway Archives)

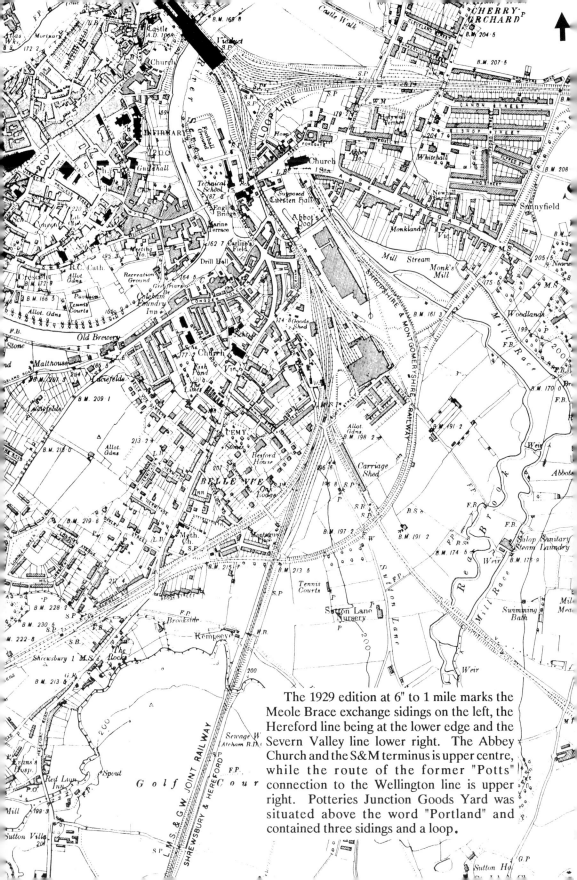

The 1929 edition at 6" to 1 mile marks the Meole Brace exchange sidings on the left, the Hereford line being at the lower edge and the Severn Valley line lower right. The Abbey Church and the S&M terminus is upper centre, while the route of the former "Potts" connection to the Wellington line is upper right. Potteries Junction Goods Yard was situated above the word "Portland" and contained three sidings and a loop.

SHREWSBURY ABBEY FOREGATE

11. The Mayor of Shrewsbury, Major Wingfield, performed the opening ceremony from the top of one of the freshly repainted ex-MR coaches on Maundy Thursday, 13th April 1911. "Ilfracombe Goods" no. 3 *Hesperus* hauled the eight-coach special up the in 47 gradient out of the station, amidst exploding detonators and much cheering. (Colonel Stephens Railway Archives)

Diagram to show the spur between the S&M oute and the Severn Valley Line that was dded in 1960 to allow tankers to reach the oil lepot at Abbey Foregate.

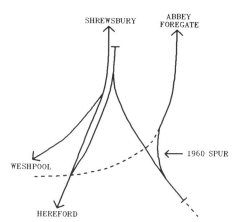

SHREWSBURY

ABBEY FOREGATE

WESHPOOL

HEREFORD

← 1960 SPUR

The 1882 survey has the PS&NWR at the top, with the connection to Potteries Junction upper right. Abbey Foregate station is upper left, the "Potts" engine shed being shown nearby. A line runs from it to a turntable which is also linked to a fan of tracks leading into the

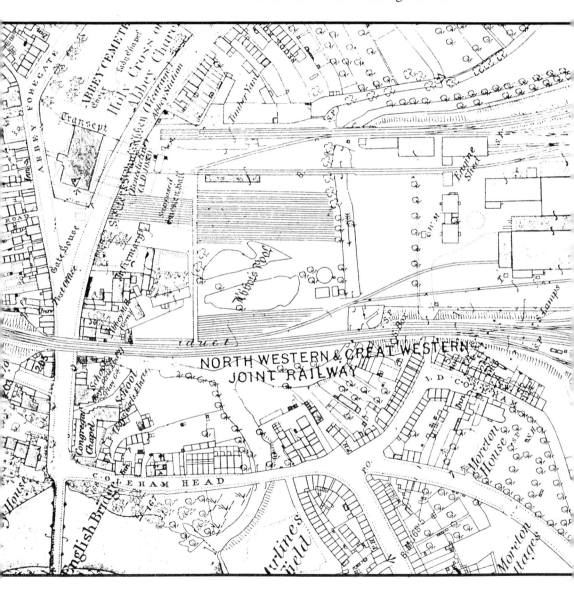

Midland Carriage & Wagon Works, which was not associated with the Midland Railway. The engine shed on the right was that of the LNWR, while their carriage shed was lower right.

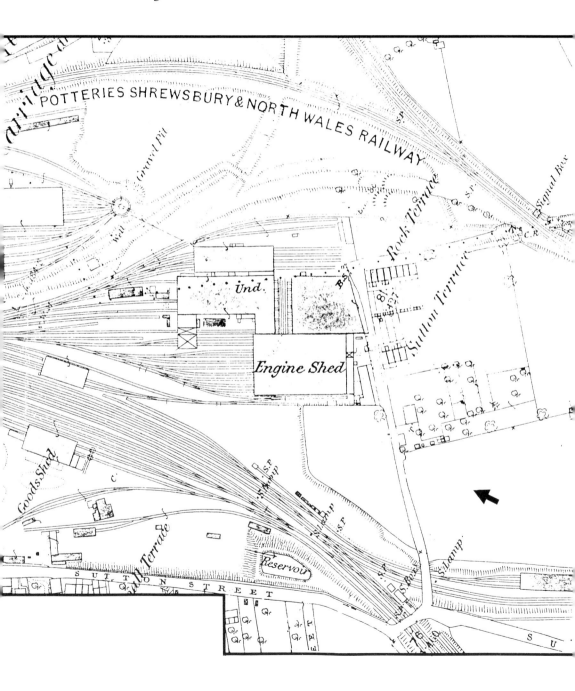

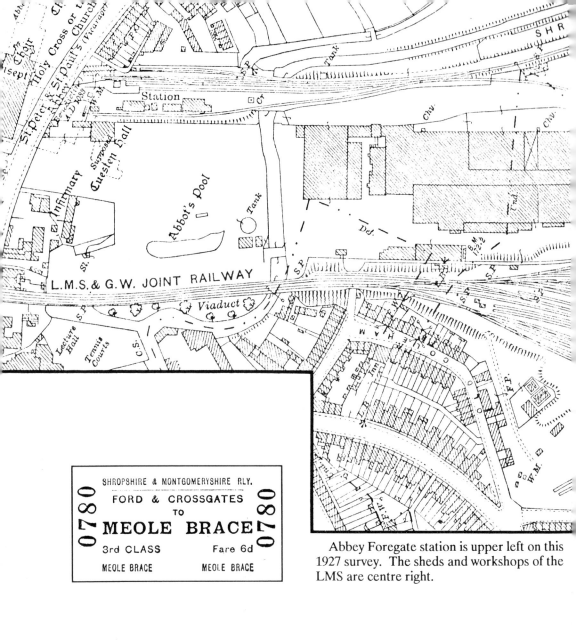

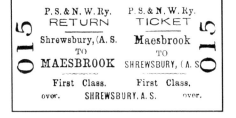

SHROPSHIRE & MONTGOMERYSHIRE RLY.

FORD & CROSSGATES
TO
MEOLE BRACE

3rd CLASS   Fare 6d

MEOLE BRACE   MEOLE BRACE

0780   0780

Abbey Foregate station is upper left on this 1927 survey. The sheds and workshops of the LMS are centre right.

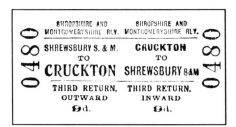

P. S. & N. W. Ry.   P. S. & N. W. Ry.
RETURN   TICKET

Shrewsbury, (A. S.   Maesbrook
TO   TO
MAESBROOK   SHREWSBURY, (A. S.

First Class.   First Class,
over.   SHREWSBURY, A. S.   over.

015   015

SHROPSHIRE AND   SHROPSHIRE AND
MONTGOMERYSHIRE RLY.   MONTGOMERYSHIRE RLY.

SHREWSBURY S. & M.   CRUCKTON
TO   TO
CRUCKTON   SHREWSBURY S&M

THIRD RETURN.   THIRD RETURN.
OUTWARD   INWARD
9d.   **9**d.

0480   0480

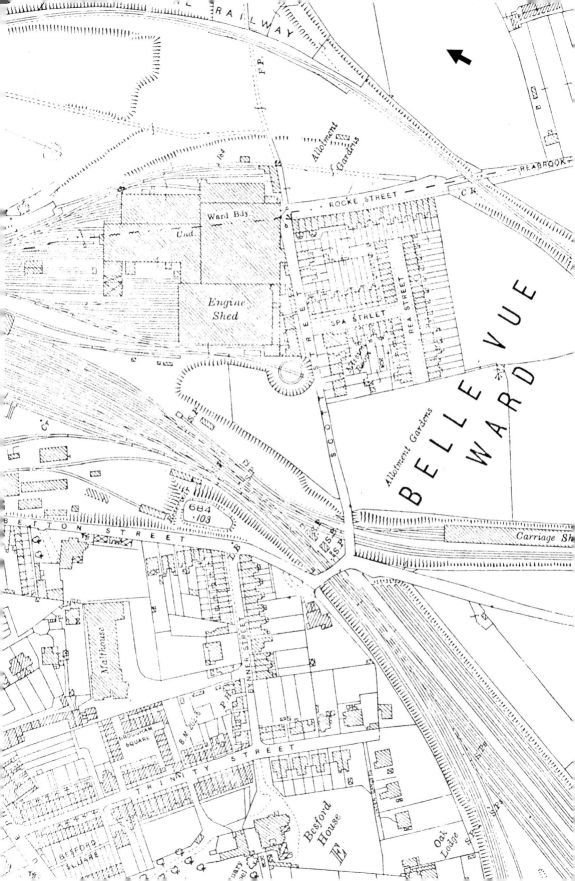

RAILWAY

F.P.

Allotment Gardens

REABROOK

ROCKE STREET

C R

Ward Bdy.

Und.

SPA STREET

REA STREET

STREET

Engine
Shed

BELLE VUE

WARD

Allotment Gardens

SCOTT STREET

684
.103

B R

F S P

F S P

Carriage Sh

BETTON STREET

Malthouse

BYNNER STREET

P H

B.M. 202·6

BROUGHAM
SQUARE

TRINITY STREET

Besford
House

Oak
Lodge

BESFORD
SQUARE

112.   The serene Abbey Church forms the backdrop to another noisy crowd scene, as country folk emerge from a busy train, baskets in hand and every head covered. The coaches nearest the camera were ex-North Staffordshire Railway.
(Colonel Stephens Railway Archives)

113. Passengers entered by the small gate on the left, the gateway on the right being to the goods yard in this 1931 view. The boundary had been established in 1837, when Telford built a new road south of the Abbey as part of the London-Holyhead road improvements, destroying much of the remains of the Abbey Refectory. (R.K.Cope/R.S.Carpenter)

114.   Having passed the booking office window, passengers followed this path to the platform ramp. Provision of a room for the ladies was a rarity on Stephens' railways - the bachelor provided none on his lines in South-East England. The waiting room was used by the ARP during WWII.
(L.Darbyshire coll.)

115. A 1937 view from the platform confirms that the line was still busy with freight. The sheeted vans were used for storing mainly grain and basic slag in sacks. The van bodies were later grounded at various stations on the route, and the water tower has more recently been moved to Wittersham Road on the revived Kent & East Sussex Railway. (R.K.Cope/R.S.Carpenter)

116. "Collier" no. 8236 is prepared for one of its rare passenger workings - an excursion on 5th August 1935, and is seen attached to an ex-MR coach. While the rural population remained almost static during the passenger carrying life of the S&M, the figures for Shrewsbury rose from 29,000 to 36,000, increasing the potential day tripper traffic. (H.F.Wheeller)

Shropshire and Montgomeryshire Railway.

Shrewsbury Great Floral Fete

Wednesday & Thursday, Aug. 16th & 17th, 1933

CHEAP EXCURSION TICKETS

Will be issued from the undermentioned Stations, by all Trains,
TO SHREWSBURY (ABBEY STATION) as below:

FROM			Return Fare 3rd Class.
Llanymynech	....	....	1/8
Maesbrook	....	....	1/6
Kinnerley	....	....	1/4
Nesscliffe and Pentre	....	....	1/2
Shrawardine	....	....	1/-
Ford and Crossgates	....	....	8d.
Meole Brace	....	....	2d.

Available to return by any Train on day of issue only.

The ordinary Train Service will be cancelled on these two days and the following Trains will run.

Up Trains			a.m.	a.m.	p.m.	p.m.
Llanymynech	-	-	8 10	11 30		
Maesbrook	-	-	8 15	11 35		
Kinnerley	-	-	8 35	11 50	5 45	8 30
Nesscliff and Pentre	-	-	8 43	11 58	5 53	8 38
Shrawardine	-	-	8 49	12 4	5 59	8 44
Ford and Crossgates	-	-	8 56	12 11	6 6	8 51
Meole Brace	-	-	9 15	12 30	6 25	9 10
Shrewsbury	-	-	9 30	12 40	6 35	9 20

(Wednesday only / Thursday only — p.m. columns)

Down Trains			a.m.	a.m.	p.m.	p.m	p.m.
Shrewsbury	-	-		10 0	2 0	6 45	10 0
Meole Brace	-	-		10 10	2 10	6 55	10 10
Ford and Crossgates	-	-		10 30	2 30	7 15	10 30
Shrawardine	-	-		10 38	2 37	7 22	10 37
Nesscliff and Pentre	-	-		10 45	2 43	7 28	10 43
Kinnerley	-	-	7 30	10 55	2 50	7 35	10 50
Maesbrook	-	-	7 40	11 5		7 45	11 0
Llanymynech	-	-	7 45	11 10		7 50	11 5

(Wednesday only / Thursday only — p.m columns)

All Trains stop by Signal to pick up and set down Passengers at intermediate Halts on notice being given at Station or to Guard on joining Train.

Shrewsbury,
July, 1933.

JAMES RAMSAY,
Managing Director.

117. Part of the fleet of six S&M cattle wagons
stand in the bay, while barrels and parcels
loiter on the platform. In the adjacent yard
Greenwood's Sentinel DG4 appears as an
example of the emerging road competition,
this vehicle collecting grain direct from the
farmer's yard. The unusual station entrance is
clear in this view. (R.Shepherd coll.)

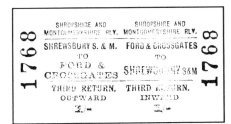

118. Vagg & Co commenced a competitive bus service to Kinnerley in 1925 and extended to Llanymynech in 1931, soon carrying 500 passengers a week. Greenwood had seven charabancs for excursions - one is visible on the right. Destinations included Blackpool - incomparable with Crew Green. This is the view from the former royal saloon at the rear of a departing excursion in 1935, the parapet railings of the bridge over the Rea being visible. (H.F.Wheeller)

19. When the Shropshire Railways commenced their abortive reconstruction of the line in 1890, the Rea bridge was rebuilt at a higher level and the entire station site was raised by several feet, to reduce the problem of flooding. A local coal merchant's wagon stands on the line to the former Midland Carriage & Wagon Works in 1937. Their premises were adapted for the maintenance of commericial vehicles.
(R.K.Cope/R.S.Carpenter)

120. WD no. 188 prepares to leave for Kinnerley, after working the SLS special on 21st September 1958. A farewell tour was arranged by the same organisation on 30th March 1960, using "Austerity" 0-6-0ST no. 193 and two coaches. (J.J.Smith)

121. The Anglo-American Oil Co. established a depot adjacent to the station in 1934, trains serving it reguarly until 15th July 1988. Thereafter, five tankers were retained for storage and fitted with handrails. The 3-ton capacity crane remained as a monument to the Stephens era and is seen on 7th August 1990, when car park construction was started on the site. The relic was rescued twelve days later for private preservation, and all the oil tanks, together with the track on which they stood, were removed shortly after. (V.Mitchell)

MP Middleton Press

Easebourne Lane, Midhurst. West Sussex. GU29 9AZ
(0730) 813169

Other similar albums featuring lines built by Colonel Stephens are shown in bold typeface.

Write or telephone for our latest booklist

BRANCH LINES

BRANCH LINES TO MIDHURST
BRANCH LINES AROUND MIDHURST
BRANCH LINES TO HORSHAM
BRANCH LINES TO EAST GRINSTEAD
BRANCH LINES TO ALTON
BRANCH LINE TO HAYLING
BRANCH LINE TO TENTERDEN
BRANCH LINES TO NEWPORT
BRANCH LINES TO TUNBRIDGE WELLS
BRANCH LINE TO SWANAGE
BRANCH LINES TO LONGMOOR
BRANCH LINE TO LYME REGIS
BRANCH LINE TO FAIRFORD
BRANCH LINE TO ALLHALLOWS
BRANCH LINES AROUND ASCOT
BRANCH LINES AROUND WEYMOUTH
BRANCH LINE TO HAWKHURST
BRANCH LINES AROUND EFFINGHAM JN
BRANCH LINE TO MINEHEAD

SOUTH COAST RAILWAYS

CHICHESTER TO PORTSMOUTH
BRIGHTON TO EASTBOURNE
RYDE TO VENTNOR
EASTBOURNE TO HASTINGS
PORTSMOUTH TO SOUTHAMPTON
HASTINGS TO ASHFORD
SOUTHAMPTON TO BOURNEMOUTH
ASHFORD TO DOVER
BOURNEMOUTH TO WEYMOUTH
DOVER TO RAMSGATE

SOUTHERN MAIN LINES

HAYWARDS HEATH TO SEAFORD
EPSOM TO HORSHAM
CRAWLEY TO LITTLEHAMPTON
THREE BRIDGES TO BRIGHTON
WATERLOO TO WOKING
VICTORIA TO EAST CROYDON
TONBRIDGE TO HASTINGS
EAST CROYDON TO THREE BRIDGES
WOKING TO SOUTHAMPTON
WATERLOO TO WINDSOR
LONDON BRIDGE TO EAST CROYDON

COUNTRY RAILWAY ROUTES

BOURNEMOUTH TO EVERCREECH JN
READING TO GUILDFORD
WOKING TO ALTON
BATH TO EVERCREECH JUNCTION
GUILDFORD TO REDHILL
EAST KENT LIGHT RAILWAY
FAREHAM TO SALISBURY
BURNHAM TO EVERCREECH JUNCTION
REDHILL TO ASHFORD
YEOVIL TO DORCHESTER
ANDOVER TO SOUTHAMPTON

LONDON SUBURBAN RAILWAYS

CHARING CROSS TO DARTFORD
HOLBORN VIADUCT TO LEWISHAM
KINGSTON & HOUNSLOW LOOPS

STEAMING THROUGH

STEAMING THROUGH EAST HANTS
STEAMING THROUGH SURREY
STEAMING THROUGH WEST SUSSEX
STEAMING THROUGH THE ISLE OF WIGHT
STEAMING THROUGH WEST HANTS

OTHER RAILWAY BOOKS

GARRAWAY FATHER & SON
LONDON CHATHAM & DOVER RAILWAY
INDUSTRIAL RAILWAYS OF THE S. EAST
WEST SUSSEX RAILWAYS IN THE 1980s
SOUTH EASTERN RAILWAY

OTHER BOOKS

MIDHURST TOWN THEN & NOW
EAST GRINSTEAD THEN & NOW

WALKS IN THE WESTERN HIGH WEALD
TILLINGBOURNE BUS STORY

MILITARY DEFENCE OF WEST SUSSEX
BATTLE OVER SUSSEX 1940

SURREY WATERWAYS
KENT AND EAST SUSSEX WATERWAYS
HAMPSHIRE WATERWAYS